THE COUPONING GUIDE:

A MOM'S GUIDE TO COUPONING

By Monica Van Zandt

Copyright ©2012 by Monica Van Zandt

All rights reserved. Reproduction and distribution are forbidden. No part of this publication shall be reproduced, stored in a retrieval system, or transmitted by any other means; electronic, mechanical, photocopying, recording, or otherwise, without written permission from the publisher.

This publication is designed to provide accurate and authoritative information with regard to the subject matter covered. It is sold with the understanding that the author and the publisher are not engaged in rendering legal, intellectual property, accounting, or other professional advice

The author and distributor individually or corporately, do not accept any responsibility for any liabilities resulting from the actions of any parties involved.

Table of Contents

1) Introduction

2) Just What Is Couponing?

3) Rules for Coupons

4) Different Kinds of Coupons

5) Coupon Finding Strategies

6) Organizing Your Coupons

7) Pro Tips and Advanced Techniques

8) The ULTIMATE Resource Page

Introduction

I would like to personally thank you and give a wholehearted welcome to a little hobby of mine called couponing. I became a "Couponer" about four years ago, right after I had my second son. We found ourselves in baby mode again, going through the usual stuff like diapers, formula, etc. I had always saved a few coupons here and there on baby stuff, but never focused on collecting or organizing them.

One day, I was at the grocery store picking up another can of Good Start formula, when a woman stopped me. She asked if I had a coupon for a can Enfamil since she happened to forget hers. By dumb luck, I actually had one on a page of coupons I was carrying in my purse. I took it out and gave it to her. She was so thankful; she handed me a coupon for the brand of baby wipes I used. I was able to trade up a few coupons that afternoon and save four dollars.

The woman explained to me that her circle of friends actually trade and share coupons together. She told me that she saved at least two hundred a month by shopping and budgeting with coupons. I could not believe it. Was this really true? Could I save that much a month?

At the time, I was not working and staying home with the boys. Two hundred a month would be a huge boost on the monthly budget and extra cash in our pockets. That extra income would be very helpful while we were going through baby mode. I was intrigued with this "couponing" thing.

That was the first time I started into coupons, to see if I could save two hundred a month. I wanted to see if I could free up extra money budgeting, spending smart, and using all of my coupons at the store.

I started doing some research reading several online blogs about couponing. I wanted to learn a little bit more about it. Soon, I was getting active in online forums talking and asking questions. This really started to get my interest because I had no idea there was so much more to this than cutting out the Sunday paper inserts.

Soon, I realized how much fun this was learning all about the hints and tricks of this hobby. I learned about doubling coupons, downloading e-coupons, and pairing up store and manufacturer items. I started looking for several online sources to learn all about what people were doing to save money.

To be honest, I think this is more like playing a game. Looking and hunting for the right deal to come out with huge savings. Originally, I was just trying to be thrifty and save a few hundred dollars a month, but it turned into a fun hobby!

I really believe you will love taking this up as a hobby. It is so gratifying to look at your receipt and see huge savings. One of the great benefits of couponing I have enjoyed is becoming very smart with our monthly budget. Couponing forces you to maintain a budget and become a frugal spender.

Now, are you wondering did I manage to save two hundred my first month jumping into coupons? Well, the answer is no. I did not reach my goal, but I was close. I had quite a bit to learn about the whole coupon business. I read and ask questions on forums for months. I had to learn by trial and error at the store. Overall, I gained a ton of experience just on my own.

I wanted to write this book so that I could share with you my experiences and help you on your way to success. This is one of my favorite hobbies; I truly have a passion for it. I hope I can give you great advice on couponing that will give you the confidence and knowledge to take this up as a hobby as well.

Just What Is Couponing?

Do you remember the "good ole' days" when life was much easier? We would get the weekend paper with that insert of coupons hidden deep within. I remember my mom would cut those out at the table, sort into two piles and later on after church it was off to the grocery store. We would go out in our Sunday's best, prodded up and down the aisles pushing the cart.

My mother was very conscious about saving every penny and never was a frivolous spender. She always made sure my sisters and I were treated well, even to the point of being spoiled a bit (grin). She always planned every meal for the week, and knew exactly what she needed. Those were the days when things were simple, just take out the coupon from the paper and go to the store.

Today's "Couponing" is something completely different. Gone are the days of clipping a coupon from the Sunday paper and savings fifty cents. The whole art of couponing has evolved into a system that you use to find the best offering of coupons, find items on sale, buy extremely low, then stock up on stuff.

Couponing has turned into a game, or as I call it my hobby. I treat it like a one; it is something I do for a few hours to relax myself. Many people go overdo it, almost become obsessive compulsive on it. The "Extreme Couponers" are the wacko and nut jobs you might catch or see on the cable TV show. You do not need to spend all of your waking time looking, hunting, and obsessing over coupons. There is much more to life than that. So, make it a fun little hobby like I do. You will get relaxation organizing your coupons, and have gratification on saving extra money at the store.

Another side note to the "Extreme Couponers" and the television show: The TV show you see is dramatized and overblown for TV. By far, all of the grocery stores have policies on couponing that would never allow these "Extreme" people to do the stuff. It is junk is scripted for TV. Most of the television show is fake. The producers will choose a store to film and take it over. Then they will instruct the cashiers and managers to allow or change store policies normally in place. It becomes a made for TV experience inside the store. Your shopping trip will not take $500 worth of groceries down to $6.65 with coupons. This is just not the reality of it.

The key to couponing is to get the items at the right time when the items go on sale at the store, and keep a supply handy until you can get it cheap again. The goal of couponing is never pay the regular price for about 80% of your items.

The general steps to achieve these awesome savings are to wait until you can get the item on sale at the right time. You will then use your coupons to buy at a low price. Then you buy one or two extra of the items (non-perishable) and keep a stockpile of it. By the time you run out of some of these items, they will go back on sale again. You start again by buying at the sale price with coupons again. It is that simple, kind of like: Wash, Rinse, Repeat.

Find the right time

The trick to couponing is to wait on items until they go on sale at the store. You can use your coupons strategically to get the best price possible. This just takes some good timing, a pinch of luck, and some organization. What Couponers will do is collect up the coupons, organize them into a system where they can plan their shopping.

My system works like this: I will cut out some of the coupons and refresh a coupon binder I store these in. I get the sales ads in the middle of the week, and I search these for items on my shopping list. If I see something on sale in the ads that we use a bit, I will check my book to see if the item has a coupon for it. If I do have one or more then I will pull it out and place it in an envelope or plastic bag. I add a checkmark next to my list to tell me I have coupons for it. When I go to the store, I have my shopping list and my baggie of coupons.

Stockpile your items

The next part of couponing is to stockpile your items you buy. What I mean by this is having a stash of things you buy with coupons while the item is on sale. Therefore, you stock up on stuff that you will use for some time until that item will go on sale again.

Here is an example about stockpiling:

I have three coupons for deodorant that I can get .75 cents of the price. The deodorant goes on sale for $2.00. I will use all of the coupons and buy three of the deodorants for $1.25 each. This makes my grand total for these three things $3.75 (plus tax). That is close to the same price you would pay when it is not on sale. I will put these in my stockpile, and use it when I need it. These three might last about 6 months or so, until I see the same thing go on sale again and I have coupons.

Essentially, my stockpile keeps me stocked up with low priced items we bought while on sale. Once you start doing this with several things, the cost start to add up quickly. When you tally up all of the items we avoid spending full price, you start to see the extra money in savings.

Can you reach that $200 per month in savings doing the coupons? Yes!

Rules for Coupons

Couponers are generally a welcoming and caring group of people. They are always looking for great deals and want to help pass that on to their fellow shoppers. Most of us rely on the manufacturers coupons to keep great savings on the items we buy. I would say most of the Couponer's understand the rules and policies the stores have created.

Since the airing of the TV show Extreme Couponing, stores have realized they have to create policies to prevent losing money. Most grocery stores operate on razor thin margins so they had to put rules in place to stay profitable. These policies and rules are in place to protect the business. Abusing these policies is a great way to ruin any future deals for all of us.

Couponing can be a rewarding experience for people who are honest and show proper etiquette. Here are some basic rules you should follow when practicing the art of couponing:

Know the stores coupon policy before shopping

One of the most aggravating things can be standing in a long line backed up because someone is arguing about coupons. This is extremely frustrating when they do not know the store policy on them. Be sure to ask a manager or help desk before going shopping on the policies of the store. Each store will be different; there is no universal law of the land.

Some stores have a cap on the amount of like coupons a customer can use or how many the store will double. In addition, some companies such as Proctor & Gamble recently changed their policy to allow no more than four like coupons in one shopping trip. The policy from store to store can also be different even for large chains like

Kroger. For example: in the suburbs of a major city, most Kroger stores double up to $1, meaning any coupon $0.50 or less will be doubled. However, outside this metro area, some stores double up to $2, meaning any coupon $1 or less will be doubled.

Some privately owned stores do not double or triple coupons at all. Be sure to read the stores website for their policy on coupons before you go shopping. If you cannot get access to the website, just go and ask a manager at the courtesy counter prior to shopping.

Read what the coupon says

When you are organizing your coupons before going shopping, be sure to read exactly what the coupon's product is. A common mistake many people make is not reading the fine print, and understanding what the coupon is savings. For example: You have a coupon for a 9oz of dish soap, you cannot use that on a 40oz bottle.

You cannot use multiple coupons

Most stores will not allow you to use two or more coupons on a single item. The only multiple coupons you can double up is the store's and the manufacturers. You cannot take two, three, or four store coupons and use them on one single item. Read the fine print on the coupon, it will tell you the exact rules.

Take what you need

When a store has an onsite coupon like a tear pad, just take what you need. You do not need to horde ten or more of these coupons. Be considerate and leave some for other shoppers. Nothing can be more annoying than an empty tear pad because some hoarder wants to save twenty cents on thirty bottles of mustard.

Never photocopy a coupon

This one is a slippery slope I tend just to avoid. I do print out coupons online, which can be tracked by the bar code and those will be ok. You cannot photocopy a manufacture's coupon out of the Sunday paper's insert. Photocopying can be considered retail fraud.

Shop on the off hours

This is a common courtesy for people waiting in line. Try to shop when the store is not so crowded with people. If you have a few hundred dollars with of groceries and a stack of coupons, it is going to take some time for the cashier to scan through them. This just backs up the line, puts a lot of stress on the cashier, and gets people very aggravated. I hate it when people do that because it gives us Couponers a bad image.

When getting into line, check to see if someone behind you has fewer items. I like to let people go in front of me because I might take some time. This just helps keep the line from backing up too much, and keeps people from getting aggravated.

Never argue with the cashier

If there is a problem that comes up while processing your coupons, ask nicely and see if you can get a clarification. If the cashier cannot help you, you can ask the head cashier or manager if they are around. Never stay and argue in line, it just backs up the line and really makes people mad behind you.

If there is a problem, the best thing you can do is go to the service desk and work it out. Use the customer service desk. Politely ask the manager at the service desk about the problem and see if they have clarification. If not, be sure to thank them for helping out as best as they can. You can follow up with a call to the owner or regional manager. Politely ask for more clarification, they will be able to help you on the issue. Keep it professional, you will be surprised how sometimes people are willing to go the extra step for you if you treat then good.

I have seen people hooting, hollering, and making a scene in line before. It is embarrassing and frankly gives couponing a bad image.

Never steal the inserts out of the newspaper

I have bought a paper, brought it home, and the insert was missing! That can be so aggravating. People are taking the coupon inserts out of the paper and stealing them. This is becoming common in stores lately. Do not be dishonest and steal, it is not worth saving just a few dollars over. If caught, you can get in trouble for shoplifting.

Do not be a hoarder

When you see these extreme Couponers on television, it is very disturbing seeing their behavior being glamorized on TV. You see them clearing out shelves of items using the coupons to get it for pennies or free. I do not consider them a Couponer; they are hoarders. Be considerate of other shoppers and take only what you need. Do not be greedy and take all of the items off the shelves because you can get it for pennies.

Always be ready to pay

When you have been standing in line for some time while the cashier processes your coupons, be prepared ahead of time to pay. I like to have my purse ready with the check prewritten out so I am not wasting time fumbling around. Nothing can be more aggravating for people waiting in line than seeing someone dilly-dallying around.

Be polite to the cashier

Even if you are having a bad day, you should be courteous to the cashier. He or she will have to process and scan through all of the coupons, which will take time. This can start to back the line up and put pressure on them to keep it moving. This can be very stressful on them as well. Sometimes there can be a computer glitches or not reading the coupons right, it is not the cashiers fault. Be kind to them and they will be sure that you get the problem fixed.

Different Kinds of Coupons

Coupons can come in many different forms. I will explain most of the basic ones here in this section. I know there is a TON more different ways you can get a discount, savings, etc. There is simple just not enough room in the book to list them all!

We will stick with the basics and go through some of the coupons that are easy to get.

Manufacturer coupons

The manufacturer creates and issues these coupons. They want to entice you to buy their brand. Found in newspaper inserts, online, and packaged within the product itself. Many of these can include both product and service.

Monthly Local Mailing

These coupons are bulk mailed to the community. They come once a month in a collection of local companies offering services and products with nice coupons in them. These are usually local companies offering good deals.

In the picture above shows some of discounts inside the coupons that arrived at my house for the month. I this local mailing had coupons for various services locally and some discounts on restaurants. I took advantage of a coupon for 15% off a bill at local buffet that just opened. I have to admit, it was good too (the food that is).

Store coupons

These are coupons issued by store (can include name brands or store brand products). The store sends these out to entice customers to keep returning. These can be located inside inserts and sales ads and found online. If you belong to a rewards club or membership to that store, they might mail special coupons directly to you.

Rebates: Mailed in to receive money back

These are discount percentages back. Many companies love to use rebates as their way to entice people to buy the products. These percentage discounts: Restaurants, clothes, entertainment, and electronics. This usually means you have to go through the rigorous steps of clipping the UPC, filling out an information card, and clipping part of the receipt. Companies love this approach because half the time people will forget or do not feel like going through the hassle of the rebate. Be sure you do not forget about this, many of these rebates also have an expiration time with it.

Digital coupons

These coupons are loaded or clipped to an online account. These will automatically deduct when you shop and pass through the register. Usually these digital coupons ties into the rewards programs the store or manufacturer offers. To get or load the coupons to your account, you will have to log online and select what ones are available.

Some of the coupons will allow you to print, some you can apply to your online account. In the picture below, I just selected a coupon to print through the Target online site.

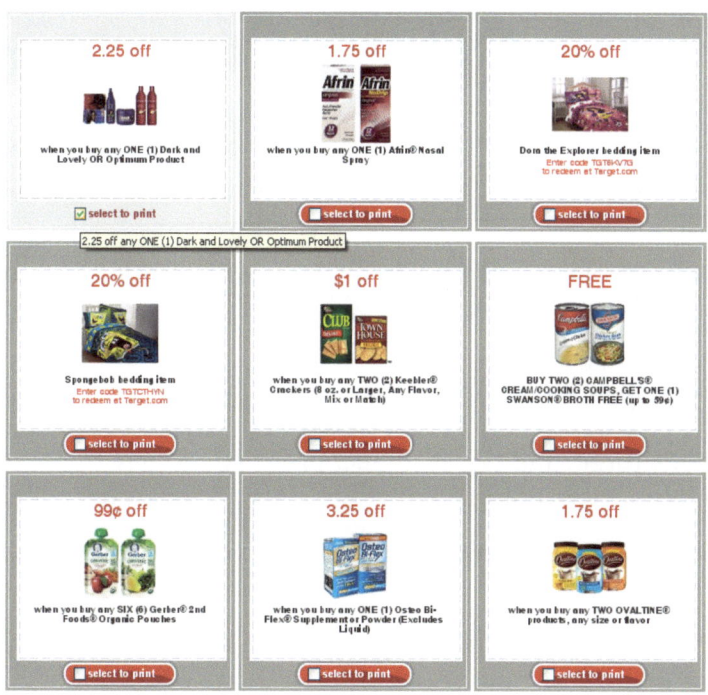

Peelies

Peelies are stickers type coupons stuck on a product in the store. When you buy the product, the coupon will come with it. The manufacturers want you to peel and keep the coupon, so you will always want to get the product again. Some places allow you to peel the sticker and use it immediately. This all depends on the policy of the store. Most places I have seen, you can just peel and use it on the spot.

In this photo above, we see a peelie sticker with a recipe and coupon inside. I could not resist, I had to check out the recipe.

Buy one get one (or two, three, etc)

The manufacturers and stores to encourage you to buy their products issue these. This works by buying one of the products, you get one free. This is a great promotion to stock up on extra items if available.

One of the products I see a lot is the Hamburger helper as buy one get one free. The price for the box is normally 4.00 per box. Guess what? You can use coupons on these as well, even during a promotion. You can buy a box with a coupon for 3.00 and get two boxes worth for that price. If you had two coupons, you can buy two boxes for 6.00 and get the additional ones free. You now have four boxes bought at 6.00, which you can put in your stockpile. Since this product does not perish for a long time, it makes an ideal thing to stock up on during these deals.

Rewards

Rewards clubs can vary between stores and programs. Essentially, the rewards programs will give you points or percent back for every level of spending you accumulate. One program I participate in is the Kroger rewards points. The more you spend at Kroger, the more you earn points towards Shell gasoline. I have accumulated enough points where I can get a 10 cent per gallon discount at the station.

Rewards have different levels and benefits. You can check online at the store for what rewards you can earn back. You can get a rewards card for your keychain that allows the cashier to get access to your account quickly.

Here is a great inside tip: I have had so many on my keychain; I had moved my cards to a single belay clip to keep on my purse. This keeps my keys free for starting my car, while the belay keeps my rewards cards attach to my purse. One quick move, I can unsnap it to get my rewards card scanned.

Coupon Finding Strategies

Half the fun of couponing is the hunt for those unusual great deals. It is like panning for gold, you are wading in the stream sifting the rocks and dirt. All of the sudden, you see a piece of color stand out against the dull river rock. Could it be? GOLD!

That is the feeling when you find that amazing and awesome coupon that is just like finding a gold nugget. It is exhilarating, fun, and when you find an offer that nobody discovered, you can share it with your fellow Couponers. It makes it fun because you were the one that hunted for it and found it first. I love being the one to send out a report on unique deals or coupons that nobody had discovered.

Here are some good strategies to finding some of the coupons. I am including ones that are easy to get, some take a bit of searching.

Weekly newspaper inserts

A study found that about 80% of the U.S. population still gets their coupons through the weekly inserts. One thing I would do is get two or more newspapers. This gives you double the amount of coupons to save on. Another strategy is to get the paper from the town our county next door. Even between the suburbs or cities, there will be different deals and values in the inserts.

If you are traveling in another region of the country, be sure to pick up the Sunday paper for the coupons. There will be coupons that target readers for that area; these will have better deals than what you would find locally.

Another great is to partner up with your neighbors and do a weekly coupon exchange. We work what products each other uses often and clip those for each other. So, every Sunday evening I stroll over to my neighbor's house drop off her coupons, then I get some in exchange. Now we double our coupons for items we use up a lot. This helps us stock up a bit on items we go through quickly.

Numerous online sites

I think I could spend hours if not weeks online, hunting around for coupons that manufacturers will place on their websites. These coupons are found online through the companies own site, or on a group blog, or through websites dedicated to producing coupons. You might find local grocery stores posting online coupons to their website that you can download.

I always search for online coupons from the local grocery store. I can stack these on the manufacturer's coupons to get a massive amount of savings. At times, I have been able to get items free doing this.

In the back of this book, I am going to provide a huge, super cool, awesome, and kick-butt reference guide to all of the blogs, online coupon sites, and much more. This will give you a good head start into joining up with the online coupon community.

Quick tip: Online coupons can only be printed a maximum of two times per computer. Therefore, here is a way to get multiple coupons beyond the two maximum. If you have a couple of laptops or desktop computers, you can install the printer file on several computers. If you print from one computer, you can do it on another one in the house.

Facebook

Facebook has fan pages of all sorts of things like people, places and things. This is a great place to look for products with a fan page. Why? You can "Like" a product and get great coupons and codes for discounts on the product. Here is a great strategy to get great deals with a ton of products while keeping your profile safe.

Start a NEW profile on Facebook. To do this, you might need to create a new email address. I would use or make a new email address you expect to fill up with ads and junk mail. The idea is NOT to use your personal email or Facebook account. We want to create a Couponer email and Facebook account! My Facebook account is Paigeisa Couponer. Funny huh?

Once you make a new account page, you can log in as your coupon name. Why do this? Simply put, you can subscribe to all the products with your Couponer name. This will keep all the ads and posts out of your own personal Facebook account!

The next thing to do is grab your grocery list or brainstorm all of your favorite products. I made up a huge list of products I like or use around the house.

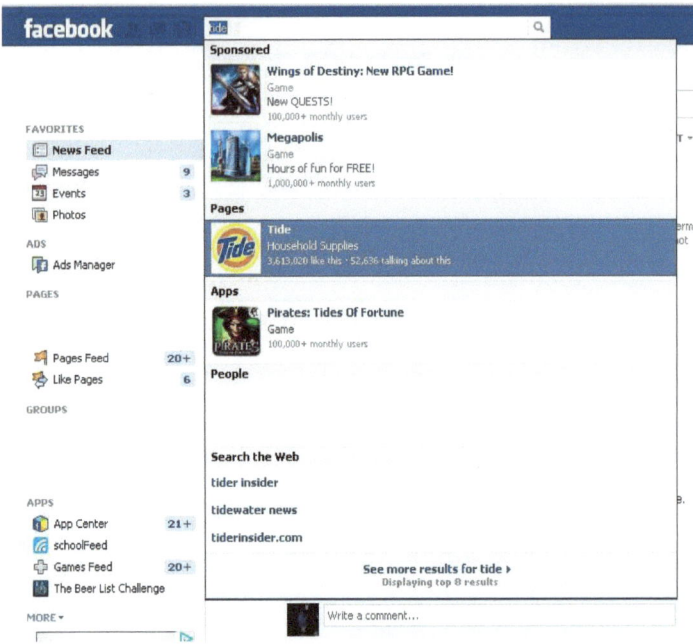

I take my list of favorite products and enter them in the search bar on the top of Facebook. If they have a fan page, it will show up in the search results. The picture here shows I typed in Tide as one of my favorites. The home page shows up, I can then click "Like" to become a fan of the page.

I will do this with several products to become the fan-page-queen! I have about 344 product "Likes" on Facebook, and get all kinds of coupons and deals. The best part of this strategy is I never get bothered on my own personal account! Awesome huh?

Coupon Booklets

Another strategy is to get involved with the various churches, clubs or organizations that run fund raising events. One of the interesting things some of the clubs do is sell a coupon book with various local businesses giving excellent deals. Usually these run about $20 to purchase and have coupons for restaurants, gym memberships, and other local shops.

Coupon books are if you go out to eat often. However, if you really don't go out much you can take advantage of the coupon book. One strategy you can use is trade bait! Offer to trade some of these restaurant coupons with your friends for goodies you can use. For example, I could ask a buy one-get one meal free coupon for two coupons for half off on ginger snaps cookies(one of my favorites).

Organizing Your Coupons

Organization is very important when you start collecting. I found that with a large collection of coupons, it is very easy to misplace them or let them expire. Most coupons have an expiration date, so they will have a limited useful time for you to use them at the store. If you do not manage your collection well, you might be taking expired coupons to the store. Now, some places might accept them even being expired. Most likely, you will feel silly in front of the cashier and not able to use half your collection.

I know that keeping things organized into a system helps you make the most worth of your coupons. Organizing the coupons into a system you feel comfortable with will help you become more efficient at planning. I never really tell people how to organize, because everyone has their own way of doing things. I will give an example of what I do here in this section, but how you run your system is strictly how you feel comfortable.

Here are some examples of how most of us store our coupons when organizing:

Binder

I love my binder! I prefer to use a binder to keep my main collection organized and up to date. I use a four-inch, three-ringed binder with inserts. The inserts have clear 3 x 3 slots to hold things the size of baseball cards. I have labeled dividers to break up each category so I can quickly flip to the one I want. It cost about $12 to buy a three-ringed binder. I found the inserts on sale that cost me about $4.30 for a package of 10. Dividers with the labels on them are super cheap. I got a pack of dividers at Office Depot for $2.00.

My binder is very precise; I have many categories labeled inside it. I can quickly find what I need, flip to it and pull a coupon. I organize my binder every Sunday, when I cut out the manufacturers coupons in the paper. I take out the ones that have expired so my book is always up to date and my collection is good.

I have categories labeled:

Produce

Salty Snacks

Fruit

Vegetables

PB & Jelly

Meats / Deli

Soups

Pasta

Breakfast

Dairy / Eggs

Sides / Rice

Freezer Goods

Drinks

Seafood

Baking Goods

Baby Stuff

Paper Products / Plastics

Spices / Oils

Dishwashing

Vitamins

Air Freshener

Pets

Misc.

First Aid

Hair Care

Beauty

Oral Care

Soaps / Lotions

Feminine Hygiene

Shaving / Deodorant

Eye Care

Summer / Sunscreen

This seems like I have a huge amount of categories, but it is well worth it when you want to be organized. Once again, I truly enjoy just sitting on the living room floor on a Sunday night, clipping and organizing. I do this after the kids are in bed and the house is somewhat quiet. My sisters do the same thing, only with a glass or wine or two!

I love my binder because I keep it extremely well organized. I am able to plan before I hit the store. The key to savings is to have a shopping list of things you need to buy in the next few weeks. I will match up the items I need to what is on sale at a store and check my binder for the coupon. Then I pull out the coupons needed for that sale at the store and place them in an envelope. Each envelope will be coupons gathered for each store to save.

CD Folder

If you are just starting out and new to doing heavy organization of coupons, you can start with a CD folder. I first started using this after I transferred all the music on my CD's to my IPOD. I had an empty CD holder just lying around, so I started stuffing it with coupons. I would organize the coupons haphazardly into the case. I found that this was useful using a CD folder was the ability to take it with you to the store. I like having the CD case with me because sometimes you find something on clearance or on sale, you did not expect. This comes in handy because that "surprise" comes along and you have a coupon waiting for it.

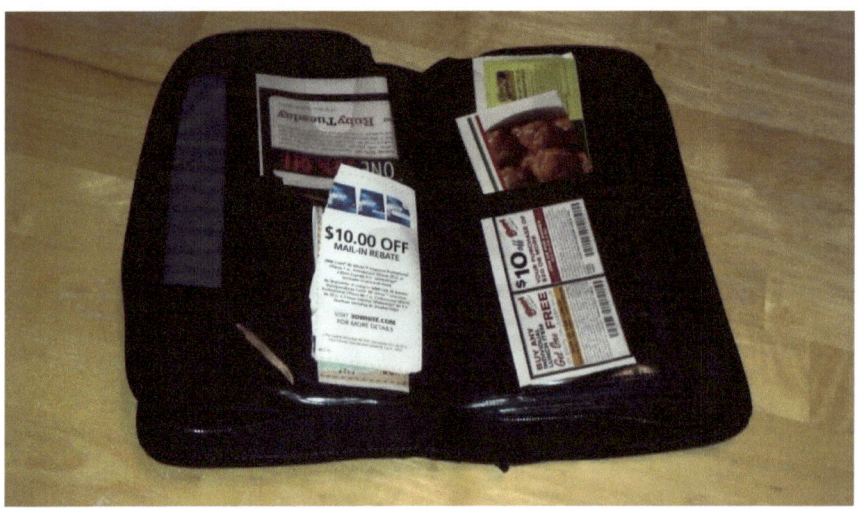

I checked online, you could find CD cases that are small and portable for around $12.00 on sites like Amazon. That is still a reasonable price if you plan to be a casual coupon collector. You do not have to lug around a large box, it does not show up as gaudy, and it does not make you look like a crazy coupon lady.

Recipe box

My mom used a recipe box and organized the tabs into categories. It was just a simple metal box from the 1960's or so. Many years ago, she used that with handwritten notecards to record family recipes passed on down through her mom. Then about fifteen years ago we had that strange thing arrived call a computer. At first, she had no clue how to use it. She started typing all of her recipes into sheets on Word Perfect. To this day, she still uses types in recipes into Word Perfect (who uses that anymore?)

That old tin sat around as a paperweight for a long time. We went shopping one day and I noticed her fumbling around through her purse at the checkout line. "Mom, did you forget your checkbook?" I asked. She responded, "Nope, can't find that darn coupon I was saving for the toothpaste". After spending an embarrassing five minutes waiting for her to search the bottomless pit called her purse, I convinced her it was a lost cause.

So, we started a new project together. I did remember that old tin recipe box and thought, what a novel idea. I explained how she could organize coupons into a file system inside the Recipe box. You take a plastic or metal box as we had and fill it with notecards. You can get those at any office supply store for 99 cents. Then we bought labeled dividers to tape to the notecards. These cost about $2.00 at the store. We wrote down basic groups like Meats, Produce, Vegetables, Candy / sweets, bathroom, kitchen. I kept it simple and easy for my mom so she could just organize the ones she needed. She does not need much groceries or supplies, so a small box like this works perfect!

Dated Inserts

Dated inserts are another way to organize your coupons to time-lapse system. As you know, most coupons only have a certain life before they expire. When you let a coupon with a great deal expire, that defeats the purpose of the collecting it in the first place. I know we get into these hectic schedules and it becomes difficult to find time to organize. I recall having a few times where I had to let it go for a few weeks. Two words can say it all: Sick boys! After that ordeal, we swing into the next one: Sick mom! After tussling around with the flu bug for a few weeks, I got into really weed out my book because I had some many of them expired.

One thing that it nice about dated inserts is this organization strategy allows you to use the coupons before they expire. In addition, this is a much simple to update and toss out all of those expired coupons. It is a complicated and somewhat time-consuming task when I weed out outdated coupons out of my binder. Here with the time elapsed binder, you know everything that is already expired by the folder. You just toss out what ones that are no good according to the label on the divider.

I tried using this organization method, but I prefer my own system. How you make this book is to create dividers. Now you can get a label maker for about $13.00 at some stores. You can print up a label and place the label on the divider. You can divide each section by one week. Start from Sunday and go out six weeks with the dividers. Sort the coupons by expiring date into each bin that is to expire that Sunday. When you go to clean out the old folder, remove the label, put the new date six weeks in advance and start over.

Pro Tips and Advanced Techniques

I surf the web quite a bit, maybe too much! When I was learning how to do it, I had to really branch out and participate in the forums. Everyone is friendly and generally loves to help any way possible. We all share this common bond between all of us. When you have a question about a strategy, there will be someone more than happy to answer it for you.

I have mentioned some of the basics of couponing, good etiquette, and good ways to organize everything. I decided to pull together this section and make it some tips and tricks I have picked up though websites, online forums, and some of my own experience. I figured this section would save you some time and make it a one stop to expert opinions.

Get a newspaper when traveling

Since many of the coupons target to regional areas, some deals might be much better than others might. These coupon inserts will be very different in other areas of the country. You can find great deals where you normally would not in your region.

Be sure to sign up for loyalty card

Many stores and retail chains have a loyalty card. This works by scanning your card and giving discounts on items for members. When you sign up, they will mail you in store coupons for being a part of the program. This is ideal to use and stack up with manufacturer coupons.

Take advantage of rebates and store reward/loyalty cards programs. CVS Extrabucks, Walgreens rewards and Rite Aid Up rewards some of the best. Many free items weekly.

Get extra newspapers

Ok. I usually get two Sunday newspapers for the coupons. If there is a bunch of great coupons on items, you might want to stock up a bit. Usually the best week for coupons is right before the holidays. Always get two or more papers around those times because the manufacturers will give great deals on holiday related foods, etc.

Keep competitors coupons

You might be shopping at one particular retail chain for items; well many stores will honor the competitor coupons. One thing you can do is check online or call ahead and ask the manager if the store has a policy on it. Many stores will honor competitor coupons; you can find great deals by stacking these on items on sale.

Super stacking coupons

I have mentioned stacking a few times, but here is an advanced way to stack on the savings. You can use both the manufacturer and the store coupon on the same item. In general, most stores honor this, but you might want to check ahead to find out if this is acceptable. Now, let us really stack them on and go extreme.

What I love to do is find an item on sale. I check my coupon binder and see if I have coupons for it. The super-stack is finding an item on sale or has a rebate, and then you stack both of the manufacturer and store's coupons on top of it.

Another way to stack on is look for the clearance rack. If you find an item about to expire or put on clearance, you can stack coupons on top of that. This is usually a hit or a miss since most of the time you do not know what on the rack. However, I have found items that I had a coupon at the time and stacked them across a clearance. I literally walked away with the item for two cents.

Think small sometimes

Many times the coupons will tell you in the fine print what sizes the product must be. Sometimes you will get lucky and they will allow any size. This is where you go small. I like to hit trial sizes or travel products with my coupons and load up with the small goods. If all goes well to this strategy, you will be able to load up with free stuff. When I see this opportunity, I like to stock up a bit with these freebies.

Go for triple savings

A few years ago, some grocery stores would allow triple coupons. This practice quickly changed after people were taking advantage of it and stores were losing money. Thanks to the TV show, stores stopped the practice and only allowed people to double then. Some stores do not even double their coupons at all. Nevertheless, in some regions the local stores still allow that. Keep an eye open for those stores. Ask around and check on the web. You might come across a store that still does this.

Write a love letter

If you truly love a product, you should write a note to the company expressing how much you value their product. Many times a company will respond back with real high value coupons for writing them. It is worth your time sending a love note to get huge savings on the product.

Follow the Pros

Some excellent bloggers out there will share insights and deals with everyone on the page. What I found is the bigger the following a blog has, the more information everyone is just dying to share with the rest online. I always love to read the blogs for information and sometimes you get a real treat with the inside scoop on something good! I found that this a great way to get freebies that nobody would have normally known.

Credit Cards

Never buy things on a credit card if you do not plan to immediately pay the balance. This is important because if you miss a payment or do not pay off the balance, you are charged the monthly interest and possibly penalties. This literally kills everything you worked for doing the coupons, because you are wasting all of that money you saved paying off the card!

Here is a good example. My friend started couponing wanting to save money. She spent hours getting her coupons organized into a book. She went to the store and started stocking up on a bunch of items. Well, she paid for it by credit card. Later on, she forgot she did that and could only afford a minimum payment. I told her she was doing it wrong, but would not listen. In the end, I had to show her she was paying more in interest on her credit card than the total she was saving with the coupons.

The ULTIMATE Resource Page

This is the ultimate resource page! I decided to collect a bunch of links and websites for you to check out. I good around on the internet quite a bit and I decided to write down my favorites places to visit. These are some great places to get online information through the blogs. You can start to chat and post with other Couponers in this friendly and fun community.

I gave some online links to where I can download coupons from the online sources. You can use these links to join up and get to sites. These give out coupons, allow you to sign up for rebates, etc. I wanted to give several links where I can print online coupons. I use these at the stores to get great deals and stack them with the local stores.

The Krazy Coupon Lady blog. Great advice and information on all levels of couponing. She lists awesome deals for the week.
http://thekrazycouponlady.com/

Couponing 101 website. This site lists weekly coupon deals at several known grocery chain stores. http://www.couponing101.com/

P&G Website. This is awesome for looking for the manufacturers coupons and where the inserts are placed in. You can do several searches and get online downloadable coupons.
http://www.pgeveryday.com

A Full Cup. More online savings and printable coupons.

Store websites like CVS, Rite Aid, Walgreens, Target, Wal-Mart, and Kmart.

Saving Star. Online source to save mostly on groceries. This has online printable coupons.

Coupons.com. Good website can download more coupons from here.

Red Plum.com. Another site like Coupons which you can download online coupons.

Smartsource.com, More online coupons that will print.

Bricks coupons. Another online website to get online coupons.

Couponnetwork.com. More printable coupons you can get.

For organic coupons: Mambosprout.com. Healthy Life Deals blog

Coupon Kindness.com donates to the charity/cause of your choice when you redeem printed coupons.

Eatbetteramerica.com. Food stuff. Mainly healthy good foods with coupons.

Couponmom.com. Another website to get online coupons to print.

HeavenlySteals.com for samples/freebie offers as well as coupon offers.

Sign up for sites such as Saving star.com which pays you back. Also ebates.com is a great store to get rewards. Reward sites to earn more coupons, free products. These include coke rewards, recycle bank, Kellogg rewards, and more.

Major chains that accept coupons include:

Target, Kmart, Wal-mart, CVS, Rite Aid, Walgreens, Trader Joes, Whole Food Market, Krogers, Albertsons, BI-LO, Meijer (Midwest), SafeWay, Sav-A-Lot, Shaw's, SuperValu, Shop 'n Save, Publix, Piggly Wiggly Food Lion, Dollar Tree, Family Dollar, and Dollar General to name a few. You can search online to locate your store and view their coupon policy.

www.ingramcontent.com/pod-product-compliance
Lightning Source LLC
Chambersburg PA
CBHW041115180526
45172CB00001B/261